J
979.4
QUA

Quasha, Jennifer

How to draw California's sights and
symbols

A Kid's Guide to Drawing America™

How to Draw
California's
Sights and Symbols

Jennifer Quasha

The Rosen Publishing Group's
PowerKids Press™
New York

To Danny and Dundeen

Published in 2001 by The Rosen Publishing Group, Inc.
29 East 21st Street, New York, NY 10010

First Edition

Book Design: Kim Sonsky
Layout Design: Michael de Guzman
Project Editor: Jannell Khu

Illustration Credits: Laura Murawski
Photo Credits: p. 7 © David Meunsch/CORBIS; p. 8 (portrait of Guy Rose and *Fly Lady* pen-and-ink sketch) courtesy of the Rose Family Collection; p. 9 © *Mist Over Point Lobos*, Guy Rose, Oil on canvas 28 ½" x 24", Morton and Donna Fleischer Collection, courtesy of Fleischer Museum. All Rights Reserved; p. 12 © 2001 One mile Up, Incorporated; p. 14 © Robesus, Inc.; p. 16 © Charles O'Rear/CORBIS; p. 18 © Tom McHugh/ California Academy of Sciences; pp. 20, 26, 28 © IndexStock; p. 22 © SuperStock; p. 24 © Tom Brakefield/ CORBIS.

Quasha, Jennifer.
    How to draw California's sights and symbols / Jennifer Quasha.
      p. cm.— (A kid's guide to drawing America)
    Includes index.
    Summary: This book describes how to draw some of California's sights and symbols, including the state's seal, the state's flag, the Golden Gate Bridge, and others.
    ISBN 0-8239-6059-5
    1. Emblems, State—California—Juvenile literature. 2. California in art—Juvenile literature. 3. Drawing—Technique—Juvenile literature. [1. Emblems, State—California. 2. California. 3. Drawing—Technique.]
I. Title. II. Series.
    2001
743'.8'09794—dc21

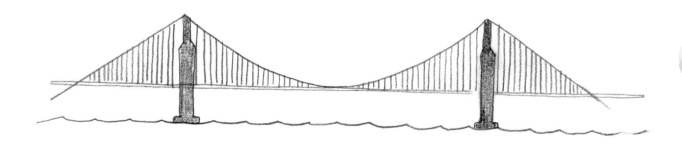

CONTENTS

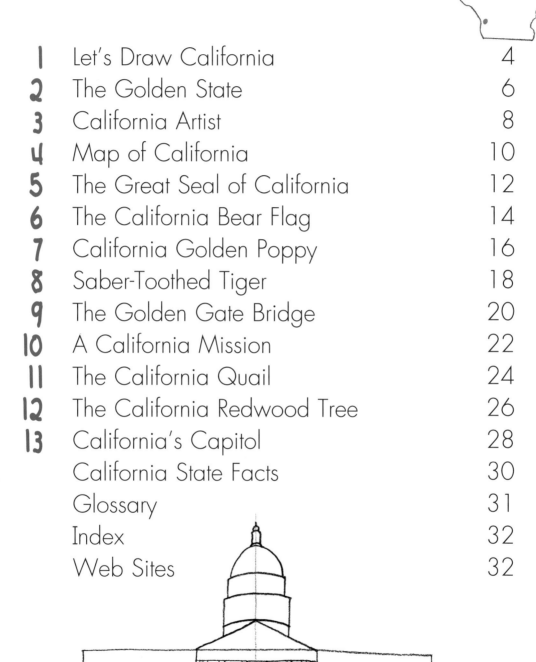

Let's Draw California

If California were its own country, it would rank sixth in the world for the number of things it produces and the amount of money it makes! This is because there are a lot of important businesses and jobs in California.

California's wealth started with its agriculture. Its major cash products are cattle, milk, cotton, and grapes. The state produces about one-third of the nation's canned and frozen vegetables and fruits. California is proud of its wines. Ninety percent of all the wine made in the United States is produced in California's Napa and Sonoma Valleys, north of San Francisco, California.

The biggest movie and entertainment industry in the world is located in Los Angeles, California. California has an important computer industry. Silicon Valley stretches for about 25 miles (40 km) in west-central California. It is called Silicon Valley because so many electronic and computer corporations set up businesses in this area in the 1970s and 1980s, and silicon chips are an important part of making computers.

This book will show you how to draw some of California's exciting sights and symbols. All the drawings begin with a simple shape. From there, you will add other shapes. Under every drawing, directions explain how to do the step. Each new step is shown in red. There are drawing terms to show you the shapes and words used throughout this book. The last step of most of the drawings is to add shading. To add shading, tilt your pencil to the side and hold it with your index finger. The more you draw, the better you will get at it. Good luck and have fun!

You will need the following supplies to draw California's sights and symbols:

- A sketch pad
- An eraser
- A number 2 pencil
- A pencil sharpener

These are some of the shapes and drawing terms you need to know to draw California's sights and symbols:

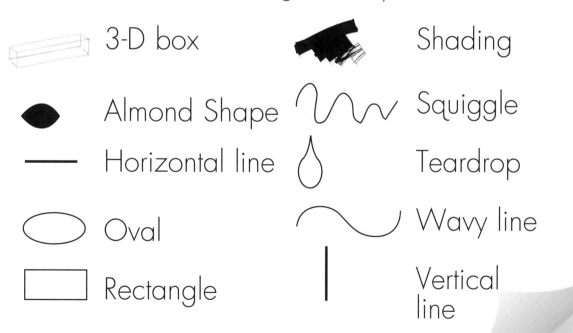

3-D box

Almond Shape

Horizontal line

Oval

Rectangle

Shading

Squiggle

Teardrop

Wavy line

Vertical line

The Golden State

California is the third-largest state in the United States. It covers more than 150,000 square miles (400,000 sq. km). Only Texas and Alaska have more land. On September 9, 1850, California was the thirty-first state to join the nation. More than 33,000,000 people live in California, more than in any other state. Los Angeles and San Francisco are the state's two most populated cities. The state capital is Sacramento. The Pacific Ocean runs along California's west coast. Mount Whitney, the highest mountain in the continental United States, is in California. The country's lowest point, Death Valley, is also in California.

In September 1542, a Portuguese navigator named Juan Rodriguez Cabrillo was the first European to set foot in what is now California. It wasn't until 1848, when a man named John Sutter struck gold, that foreigners from all over the world came to California. California is often called the Golden State because of the discovery of this precious metal.

The majestic Mount Whitney stands 14,494 feet (4,418 m) tall! It is one of the most popular mountains to climb in the United States.

California Artist

Guy Orlando Rose

Most people consider Guy Orlando Rose California's leading Impressionist painter. Impressionism was a major art movement that started in France during the late nineteenth and early twentieth centuries. Rose was born in San Gabriel, California, in 1867. He studied art in San Francisco and in Paris, France. While in Paris, Rose met the famous Impressionist artist Claude Monet. Rose liked Monet's work and began to use the same technique and style in his own work.

Rose's pen-and-ink sketch, *Fly Lady*, was done between 1888 and 1890.

When Rose returned to California in 1914, he painted many scenes set along the Pacific Coast in the Impressionist style. Rose is also known as a leading figure in the California regionalist movement. This means that his specialty was in painting California's landscapes. Painting the natural beauty of California in the state's wonderful light became a perfect way for Rose to show his love of nature.

The painting below is called *Mist Over Point Lobos*. It is a view of a rocky coastline in northern California. Rose painted the same scene many times, at different times of the day and from slightly different angles. This was how Rose's friend Monet had painted French landscapes. Although Rose died in 1925, he lives on through his art. His paintings not only show us the love he had for California, but also what the state looked like before towns and cities were built.

This is Rose's painting, *Mist Over Point Lobos*, c.1915.
Oil on canvas, 28 ½" x 24" (72 cm x 61cm)

Map of California

Map of the Continental United States

California borders three U.S. states: Oregon, Nevada, and Arizona. It also borders the country of Mexico. California has 12 regions, or areas:

- The North Coast
- San Francisco and the Bay Area
- Central Valley
- Central Coast
- Los Angeles County
- Orange County
- San Diego County
- Shasta Cascade
- Gold County
- The Deserts
- The High Sierras
- The Inland Empire

California has the Sierra Nevada Mountain Range and four famous national parks, Death Valley National Park, Yosemite National Park, Sequoia National Park and Kings Canyon National Park. Inyo National Forest has bristlecone pine trees that are 4,700 years old, the oldest living things on Earth!

1

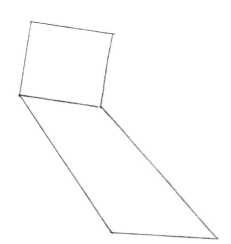

Draw a square and draw the angled shape as shown.

2

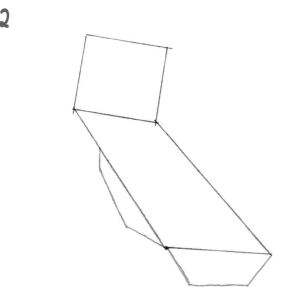

Add some angled lines as shown.

3

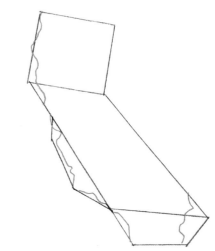

Soften or curve the angled lines. You just drew the state of California! Now let's draw some of California's important places.

4

☆ Sacramento
⟋ Sacramento River
⌂ Yosemite
∨ Death Valley
🎬 Disneyland
• Mission San Luis Rey de Francia

a. Draw a star for the capital, Sacramento.
b. Draw the V shapes as shown for Death Valley.
c. Draw a dot for Mission San Luis Rey de Francia.
d. Draw a curvy line for the Sacramento River.
e. Draw a square with a triangle on the top of it for Yosemite National Park.
f. Draw two circles and a half-moon for Disneyland.

The Great Seal of California

California's state seal was designed by R. S. Garnett, a major in the U.S. Army. It was approved in 1849, a year before California became a state. Thirty-one stars are at the top of the seal. The stars represent each state that was in the Union at the time California became a state in 1850. Under the stars is an ancient Greek word, eureka. It means "I found it" and it is a tribute to the gold miners who found gold during California's gold rush. Near the center is Minerva, the Roman goddess of wisdom. The grizzly bear, an animal native to California, is near her. A man is mining in the Sacramento River and there are ships sailing behind him. The Sierra Nevada Mountains rise high in the background.

1

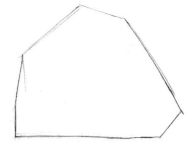

To draw one of the ships featured in the seal, begin with an angled shape. This is the overall basic shape of the boat.

2

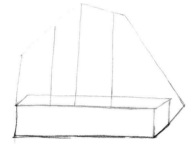

At the bottom of the shape, draw a 3-D rectangle box. Draw three vertical lines that extend from the rectangle up to the top of the shape. These are guides for the sails.

3

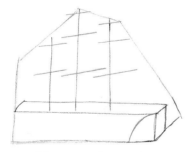

Draw a curved line on the right side of the rectangle. Add horizontal lines over the vertical lines. These lines are for the sails.

4

Use the horizontal and vertical lines as guides to draw curved, rectangular shapes. These are the sails. Erase the extra lines from the rectangle.

5

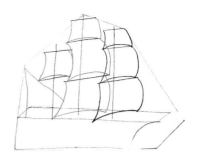

Continue drawing the sails as shown. Draw a pointy shape on the left side. This is the back sail.

6

Draw a triangle. Connect it to a curved, rectangular shape on the lower right. Draw curved lines on the rectangle.

7

Draw a triangle on the left side. Draw little rectangles on the bottom for windows. Draw horizontal lines on the bottom.

8

Draw lines on the sails to show that the wind is blowing. Shade in the middle of the bottom rectangle. Congratulations! You just finished your ship!

The California Bear Flag

The California Bear Flag became California's state flag in 1911. It is a white flag with a grizzly bear walking above the words California Republic. In the early nineteenth century, there were as many as 10,000 grizzly bears in the state. Today there are none! As the state became more populated, the grizzlies were killed for their skins and for food. In 1953, the grizzly bear became the official state animal. Above the bear, a red star sits at the top left corner of the flag. The red star is a copy of the lone star of Texas. A red border on the bottom completes the design of the flag. Today, the state flag is hung proudly in front of many schools and government buildings.

CALIFORNIA REPUBLIC

1

Draw three circles. The smallest circle is the head and the larger circles are the body.

2

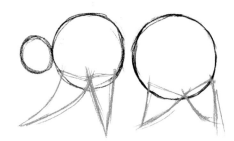

Draw upside-down triangles underneath the circles. These are the legs. Notice how some of the lines are curved and some are straight. Good job!

3

Connect all of these shapes together by drawing curved lines between the circles, shaping the body and neck. Square off the tips of the triangles to make the feet of the bear. For the mouth, draw a little rectangle on the head circle.

4

To finish the head, draw a small triangle in the rectangle for the mouth. Draw another triangle for the ear. Draw a five-pointed star as shown.

5

Draw the shape underneath the bear. Draw the border on the bottom. Write the words California Republic above the border. The last step is to either shade in the star and the border or color them in with a red pencil. Good job! You just drew the state flag!

California Golden Poppy

The California golden poppy (*Eschscholtzia californica*) is a wildflower that grows all over California. It became California's state flower on March 2, 1903. The French author and naturalist, Adelbert von Chamisso, first wrote about this flower in 1816. He was part of a scientific expedition that took place from 1815 to 1818. When his ship landed in San Francisco in October 1816, these poppies were among the few plants still in bloom. Chamisso named the flower in honor of Johann F. Eschscholtz, the ship's physician.

In the movie *The Wizard of Oz*, Dorothy and all of her friends fall asleep in a poppy field by the side of the yellow-brick road! Long ago, Native Indians used poppies for food and in medicines.

1

Begin by drawing a curved, upside-down triangular shape. This is the bulb.

2

On the bottom of the bulb, draw a small rectangle. Then draw another smaller, upside-down triangle. Extend the point of the triangle until you have a straight line coming down the page.

3

Draw a skinny *S* in the middle of the bulb. Extend and curve the top of the *S* toward the right. Draw a *C* shape on the other side of the flower. These are the outer petals.

4

On top of the bud, draw an egg shape that's turned on its side. This is the inner petal. Draw a line that extends from the stem on the lower right and loop it back, making a paddle-like shape. This is the bud.

5

Erase where the egg shape overlaps the front petals. Draw a wavy line in the bud. Add a diagonal line underneath the wavy line in the bud. Add the leaves by drawing lines that extend out from the stem. Draw the lines on either side of the stem.

6

Great job! Shade in the areas as shown using the tip of your pencil and very lightly, line by line, shade in the areas. Add lines to the leaves. Excellent work!

Saber-Toothed Tiger

California's state fossil is the saber-toothed tiger, *Smilodon*. Saber-toothed tigers lived in the Cenozoic era, more than 65 million years ago. The *Smilodon* is not really a tiger but a mammal that is an ancestor of cats, dogs, bears, and weasels. It is called a tiger because that is the animal it looks most like today. Through these fossils, we know that the *Smilodon* was about 12 inches (30 cm) shorter than a lion, but two times as heavy. He had a long tail, called a bobtail, and two huge saber teeth. The *Smilodon* became extinct about 10,000 years ago. Thousands of *Smilodon* fossils have been found in the La Brea Tar Pits since 1912. Today you can visit the tar pits in Hancock Park in Los Angeles.

1

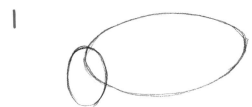

Begin by drawing a long, skinny oval. This is the body. Draw another, smaller oval to the left. This is the head.

2

Draw four circles on top of the larger oval. These will guide you when drawing the legs, in the next step.

3

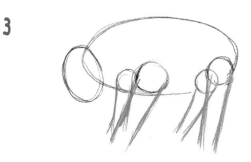

Adding on to those circles, draw lines extending down. These are the legs.

4

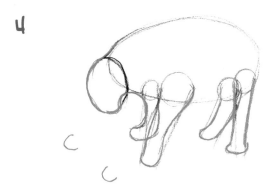

Finish the legs by connecting the lines with C shapes. Using the lines as guides, curve them to shape the legs. Draw the neck by making more curved lines as shown.

5

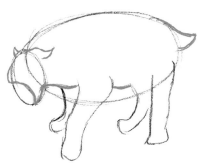

Draw pointy, triangular shapes as shown. These are the ears and tail. Draw a curved line for the mouth, which is open wide. Add curved lines on the belly. Erase any extra lines.

6

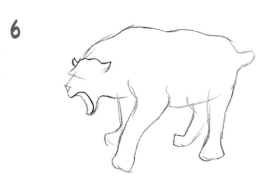

Draw a T in the middle of the face. This will guide you to draw the nose and the eyes. Draw an upside-down triangle for the nose. Draw a curved shape for the mouth.

7

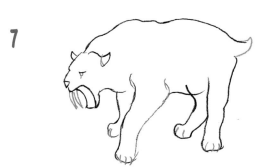

Draw in the eye as shown. Add claws to the feet. Erase extra lines. Excellent job!

The Golden Gate Bridge

The Golden Gate Bridge is one of California's most beautiful and recognizable landmarks. After four years of work, the Golden Gate Bridge was finished in 1937. It was designed by Joseph Strauss, a Chicago engineer, and cost about $35 million to build.

The bridge is 1.7 miles (2.7 km) long and connects San Francisco to Marin County. The bridge has six lanes and is 260 feet (79 m) above the San Francisco Bay. There are two red towers that rise 746 feet (227 m) off the bridge. There are two cables that run over the top of the towers, from one side of the bridge to the other. They are more than 3 feet (1m) thick and 7,600 feet (2,316 m) long. Every day 120,000 cars, buses, and trucks drive across this famous bridge!

1

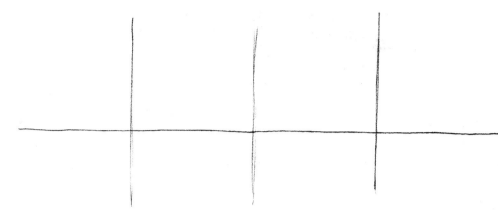

Begin by drawing a horizontal line. Divide that line with three vertical lines. Notice where those vertical lines are placed.

2

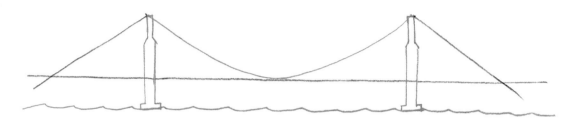

Draw another horizontal line above the first horizontal line, as a guide. Draw two triangles as shown.

3

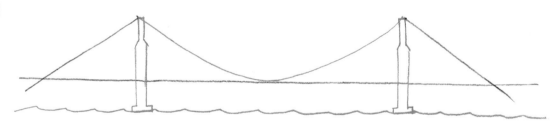

Curve the lines in the triangles in the center of the bridge. Draw in two thin shapes as shown. These are the supports. Notice how those shapes are in the center of the triangles. Draw in a wavy line underneath those shapes to show the ocean.

4

Awesome job! Add another line underneath the bridge. Shade in those tall, thin shapes. Draw straight vertical lines as shown. These are the cables.
Great job!

A California Mission

The Spanish settlers wanted to colonize California. The easiest way to do that was to set up missions. This is a place where religious leaders teach others about a religion. Between July 16, 1769, and July 4, 1823, the Spanish built 21 missions in California. The Spanish hoped to convert the Native Americans to Christianity and have them be part of the Spanish Empire. Fray Junípero Serra was one of the first missionaries in California. When he died in 1784, after founding nine missions, Fray Fermin Lasuén took his place. It was Fray Lasuén who founded Mission San Luis Rey de Francia in 1798. It is the largest of the 21 missions that are built along the coast of California.

1

To draw Mission San Luis Rey de Francia, begin by drawing a rectangle.

2

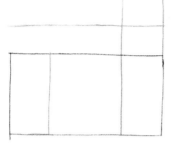

Divide the rectangle into three sections by drawing two vertical lines. The first and third sections should be the same size. Extend the lines on the right rectangle up. Draw a horizontal line that crosses the vertical lines.

3

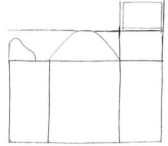

Draw a triangle above the middle rectangle. Draw a curved shape above the left rectangle. Draw a smaller rectangle within the rectangle on the upper right. Excellent!

4

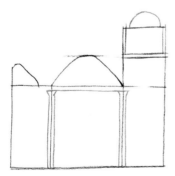

Now add a semicircle on top. Draw a line across the top of the middle box. Add two lines down on either side for columns.

5

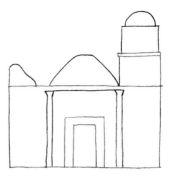

Erase the lines in the columns and in the top right rectangle. Draw a rectangle within a rectangle in the middle rectangle.

6

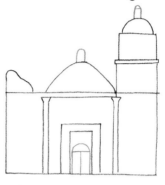

Draw in the door as shown. Draw two upside-down U shapes on top as shown.

7

Draw more upside-down U shapes as shown. Draw the circle on top of the door.

8

Draw the crosses. Add the vertical lines and the shape on top of the left rectangle.

23

The California Quail

The quail became California's state bird in 1931. The California quail is a small, round bird about 8 inches (20 cm) long. Quails have funny-looking feathers rising off the tops of their heads, called a nodding crest. The quail's head is usually black with white stripes. Though both the male and female quails' bodies are gray, brown, and white, they do not look the same. The male has many more black-and-white markings. Although quails can fly, they usually are seen walking or running on the ground. Quails are often found in groups, or flocks. Quails roost, or rest, at night. They eat seeds, plants, and insects off the ground. Quails use small plants to build their nests on the ground near trees.

1

Begin by drawing an oval. This is the body.

2

Draw a circle to the upper left. This is the head.

3

Connect the circle and the oval with curved lines. Draw a curvy triangle at the bottom of the oval. This is the body.

4

Draw the curvy shape on top of the head. This is the nodding crest. For the beak, draw a little bump on the side of the head. Now, draw in the legs underneath the body as shown.

5

Draw a little circle for the eye. Draw a line in the beak. Extend the line onto the head and neck. This is a guide for shading in the next step. Lightly draw in the wings as shown.

6

Shade in the drawing slowly and lightly, using the side of your pencil. Use the lines in the head, neck, body, and wings as guides. Great job!

25

The California Redwood Tree

California redwood trees are the tallest trees in the world. They can live for more than 2,000 years! The redwood became the state's official tree in 1937. There are two types of California redwoods, the coast redwood and the giant sequoia. At the Redwood National Park, you can find a coast redwood that is 368 feet (112 m) tall. This is the world's tallest tree. At Sequoia National Park, there is a giant sequoia tree that weighs 6,000 tons (5,443 t) and is 36 feet (11 m) wide! This is the largest tree in the world.

1

Draw a tall, thin triangle. This is the trunk.

2

Darken the shaded areas as shown. These are the branches and leaves.

3

Turn your pencil on its side and lightly shade from side to side on top of the trunk. Practice shading this way on a piece of scrap paper. Hold the pencil lightly while you stroke the paper gently. Well done! You have drawn the area of the branches and leaves.

4

Adding to the branches and leaves, draw straight and curved lines throughout the tree to add detail to the branches.

5

Finally, shade in the trunk, turning your pencil on its side again. Shade the trunk by sweeping your pencil up and down the tall trunk. Great job!

California's Capitol

The California State Capitol Building stands in Sacramento, the state's capital city. It was designed in 1860, by Miner F. Butler and Rueben Clark, and it took almost 15 years to build. When construction ended, the total cost to build the Capitol Building was $2.4 million. The architectural style of the building is called the Renaissance revival style. The building is 220 feet tall (67 m). The front of the building has eight freestanding columns. Inlaid columns also were built into the outside of the building all the way around. The Capitol has a beautiful dome, or rotunda. The governor of California works in the building with many other government officials.

1

Begin by drawing a long rectangle. This is the base of the Capitol.

2

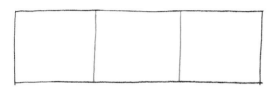

Divide the rectangle equally into three sections by drawing two vertical lines.

3

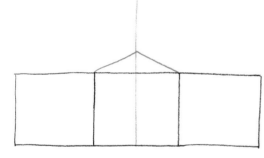

First draw a light vertical line in the middle of the center rectangle. Using this line as a guide, draw a triangle above the middle rectangle as shown.

4

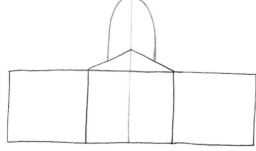

Super! Add an upside-down *U* shape on top of the triangle. This is the dome.

5

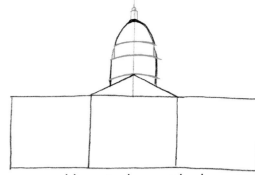

Draw curved lines in the upside-down *U* shape. Add a mini dome shape on top.

6

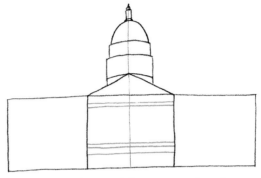

Going back to the middle rectangle, draw five horizontal lines as shown.

7

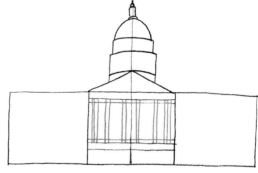

Using those horizontal lines as guides, draw vertical lines. These are the columns.

8

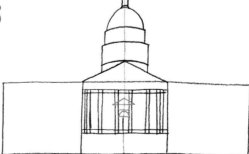

Finish with the shapes as shown. Good job!

California State Facts

Statehood	September 9, 1850, 31st state
Area	158,869 square miles (411,469 sq. km)
State Population	33,145,121
Capital	Sacramento, population, 376,200
Most Populated City	Los Angeles, population, 3,553,600
Industries	Film, electronics, computers, software, petroleum, tourism, wine
Agriculture	Vegetables, fruit, grapes, dairy products
State Animal	California grizzly bear
State Dance	West Coast swing dance
State Bird	California quail
State Flower	California golden poppy
State Fish	Golden trout
State Fossil	Saber-toothed tiger
State Tree	California redwood
State Gemstone	Benitote
State Insect	Monarch butterfly
State Marine Mammal	California gray whale
State Mineral	Native gold
State Reptile	California desert tortoise
State Rock	Serpentine
State Nickname	The Golden State

Glossary

ancestor (AN-ses-tur) A relative who lived long ago.

bobtail (BAHB-tayl) A long tail often found on cats.

Cenozoic (seh-neh-ZOH-ik) A time period more than 65 million years ago.

colonize (KAH-luh-nyz) To settle in a new land and claim it for the government of another country.

convert (kun-VURT) To change from one religious belief to another.

crest (KREST) A head decoration on a bird.

engineer (en-jih-NEER) A person who is an expert at planning and building bridges and other things.

expedition (ek-spuh-DIH-shun) A journey made for a particular reason.

extinct (ik-STINKT) No longer existing.

foreigners (FOR-in-urz) People from other countries or places.

mining (MYN-ing) Removing minerals, like gold, from the ground.

navigator (NA-vuh-gayt-ur) An explorer of the seas.

populated (PAH-pyoo-layt-ed) Having a number of people living in a place.

recognizable (reh-kig-NYZ-uh-bul) Well-known.

republic (ree-PUB-lik) A form of government in which the authority belongs to the people.

roost (ROOST) To rest and sleep.

rotunda (roh-TUN-dah) A round dome.

saber-toothed (SAY-bur TOOTHD) Having a long, sharp tooth.

technique (tek-NEEK) A method or way of bringing about a desired result in a science, art, sport, or profession.

tribute (TRIH-byoot) An act of generosity toward a person.

Index

Web Sites

To find out more about California, check out these Web sites:

www.state.ca.us
www.library.ca.gov/